HOW-TO SUNDAY SCHOOL GUIDE: CURRICULUM WORKSHOP FOR ADULT LEADERS

John McClendon

© Copyright 2004 • LifeWay Press
All rights reserved

No part of this work may be reproduced or transmitted in any form or by any means,
electronic or mechanical, including photocopying and recording, or by any information or
storage or retrieval system, except as may be expressly permitted in writing by the publisher.
Requests for permission should be addressed in writing to:
LifeWay Press, One LifeWay Plaza, Nashville, TN 37234.

ISBN 0-6331-9415-8

This book is a resource in the Leadership and Skill Development category
of the Christian Growth Study Plan for course number
LS-0036: Adult Sunday School Leadership.

Dewey Decimal Classification: 268.434
Subject Headings: SUNDAY SCHOOLS—ADULTS

Printed in the United States of America

Leadership and Adult Publishing
LifeWay Church Resources
One LifeWay Plaza
Nashville, Tennessee 37234-0175

To order additional copies of this book or other resources identified as available from LifeWay Church Resources, WRITE LifeWay Church Resources Customer Service, One LifeWay Plaza, Nashville, TN 37234-0113; FAX order to (615) 251-5933; PHONE 1.800.458.2772; E-MAIL to *CustomerService@lifeway.com;* ONLINE at *www.lifeway.com*; or visit the LifeWay Christian Store serving you.

Unless otherwise noted, all Scripture quotations are taken from the Holman Christian Standard Bible®
Copyright © 1999, 2000, 2002, 2003 by Holman Bible Publishers. Used by permission.
Scripture quotations marked (NIV) are from the Holy Bible, New International Version. Copyright © 1973, 1978, 1984 by International Bible Society.

CONTENTS

Introduction 3
Teaching for Change: Helps for the Adult Sunday School Teacher

Chapter 1 4
Gathering the Resources

Chapter 2 8
Getting Ready for Sunday's Session—Beginning Early

Chapter 3 13
Getting Ready for Sunday's Session—Studying the Lesson

Chapter 4 17
Getting Ready for Sunday's Session—Crafting an Effective Lesson

Chapter 5 25
Encountering God During the Session

Chapter 6 27
What Happens After the Session?

Chapter 7 29
For Adults With Special Needs

Procedures 30
Teaching Plan for Training Teachers

Christian Growth Study Plan 32

HOW TO USE THIS RESOURCE

- **As an individual teacher:** As you work through the chapters, you will become better prepared for the Sunday School session. Chapters 2 through 5 will show you how to assimilate lesson preparation into your weekly routine.
- **Local church training:** The 2.5-hour teaching plan in the back of the book can be used in a training setting to help teachers learn how to prepare for the Sunday School session. The plan can be modified for shorter training sessions. The teaching plan will draw heavily on the use of the entire workbook, so it is recommended that every participant have a copy.
- **State or associational training:** The 2.5-hour teaching plan can be used for training multiple churches as well. It can be used to help churches become familiar with the Adult Sunday School curriculum choices available from LifeWay how to use them effectively. The plan depends heavily on the use of the entire workbook, so it is recommended that every participant have a copy.

In addition, suggested ways to use this teaching plan, PowerPoint® helps, handouts, and other related materials available are at *www.lifeway.com/downloads/*.

Although curriculum excerpts are provided throughout the guide, it is recommended that you refer to your own copy of your curriculum as you work through each chapter.

Introduction

TEACHING FOR CHANGE:
HELPS FOR THE ADULT SUNDAY SCHOOL TEACHER

Why did you commit to teach Sunday School? How you answer this question will determine how much time you spend preparing during the six days leading up to the Sunday session. It will shape how you how you prepare your heart, your lesson, and the class for the Sunday School session.

Second Timothy 3:14-17 is a beautiful picture of why we teach—we teach for change!

> *But as for you, continue in what you have learned and firmly believed, knowing those from whom you learned, and that from childhood you have known the sacred Scriptures, which are able to instruct you for salvation through faith in Christ Jesus. All Scripture is inspired by God and is profitable for teaching, for rebuking, for correcting, for training in righteousness, so that the man of God may be complete, equipped for every good work.*

Paul, Timothy's teacher, greatly influenced Timothy's life. Timothy knew Paul and learned from him in a relationship based on integrity, accountability, and trust. What Timothy learned from Paul and others was the Word of God. This brought him face-to-face with his need for Christ, and Timothy accepted Christ through faith.

Paul challenged Timothy to continue studying the Scriptures because they are inspired by God and would impact all areas of his life. The result of continued study would be a "man of God . . . complete, equipped" to sit in the Sunday School classroom from week-to-week and absorb more information. Oops! That isn't what the Scripture says! It states that he will be "complete, equipped for every good work."

Is this what you desire to see happen in the lives of class members? They come; they hear the Scriptures taught by a teacher they know and trust; they accept Christ as their Savior; they mature; and they are readied to serve wherever God desires—even if it means they leave the class to go serve elsewhere in Sunday School. This kind of ministry is worthy of our commitment. God gives you the opportunity to experience this as a Sunday School teacher.

But how? This kind of teaching ministry requires more than preparing the lesson on Saturday night and going to church Sunday to present an outline and some interesting points. It requires intentional preparation. If you desire to guide adults to experience life-changing Bible study, then you will benefit from the training in this book. As you read, remember that God called you to teach. Therefore He will equip, guide, and bless your ministry through Sunday School. May this resource provide the tool you need to join Him in seeing lives changed!

CHAPTER 1

GATHERING THE RESOURCES

A few years ago my family and I visited the Big Island of Hawaii. We decided to visit the Hawaii Volcanoes National Park to see the lava flows from the Kilauea volcano. However, we didn't prepare for the trip. When we arrived we had not dressed for the cool wet climate. We were going to hike to the lava flows and we saw warnings all along the trail stating we needed plenty of water and flashlights—we had neither! We could see where we wanted to hike, but could not get there because we did not have everything we needed.

Let Us Help You

LifeWay's goal is to help you reach your potential as a Sunday School leader by providing excellent resources. These resources are designed to make your job easier. They do not replace the Bible, but rather assist you in understanding and using it.

Imagine creating from scratch, every week, a fresh new lesson focused on spiritual transformation and not just biblical information. After a while you would run out of ideas to sustain the interest of your class. Or you might choose a difficult topic and need a clear but scholarly explanation.

LifeWay provides doctrinally sound resources that provide for these needs. The following resources can enable you to get where you know you need to be with Adult Sunday School.

Family Bible Study

Family Bible Study offers age-group-tailored Bible studies that focus on the entire family. These Bible studies include personal-reflection and life-application questions based on a biblical worldview.

Age Groupings:
- Family Bible Study, Non Graded, King James Version
- Family Bible Study, Non Graded, Holman Christian Standard Bible®
- Life Answers for adults 18-30, HCSB®
- Life Truths for adults 31-54, HCSB®
- Life Ventures for adults 55 and up, HCSB® and KJV parallel translations

Family Bible Study Resources:
- *Leader Guides*: contain commentary, leadership helps, department assembly helps, and teaching plans for each age group
   → Adult Leader Guide KJV
   → Adult Leader Guide HCSB®
   → Leader Guides for Life Answers, Life Truths, and Life Ventures
- *Leader Packs:* contain session posters, worksheets, and a CD-ROM with leader helps
   → Adult Leader Pack
   → Leader Packs for Life Answers, Life Truths, and Life Ventures
- *Herschel Hobbs Commentary:* additional commentary help based on the KJV
- *Advanced Bible Study Commentary:* in-depth exposition based on the HCSB®
- *Sound Truths: Bible Studies on Tape:* 15-minute commentary by Calvin Miller
- *Family Bible Study Adult Audiocassette:* presents the entire text of the *Adult Learner Guide KJV*
- *Biblical Illustrator*: use for Bible background research
- *Biblical Illustrator Plus*: quarterly CD-ROM with current issue of the magazine plus related articles from the archive
- *EXTRA!*: weekly online supplement to teaching plans in printed curriculum containing current events and additional teaching options, available at *www.lifeway.com/myextra*
- *QuickSource*: two one-page teaching plans for each lesson (in addition to suggested plans in the *Leader Guides*) plus at least four audience-targeted ideas
- *Learner Guides:* for use by class members in class and for study during the week
   → Adult Learner Guide KJV
   → Adult Learner Guide KJV, Large Print
   → Adult Learner Guide HCSB®
   → Life Answers Learner Guide
   → Life Truths Learner Guide
   → Life Ventures Learner Guide
- *Christian Single Plus*: magazine designed specifically for Single Adults which includes the weekly Bible study lessons for Sunday School

Family Bible Study Resources for Special Needs:
- *Access Leader Guide:* helps leaders make spiritual preparations before they choose weekly teaching activities for those with special needs; contains personal Bible study and teaching plans
- *1st and 2nd Graders' Teaching Pictures*: contains colorful, illustrated teaching pictures related to Bible lessons that can be used with Access resources
- *Access Learner Guide:* illustrates God's love and introduces important biblical concepts through photographs, activities, music, and more, in ways that persons who have mental handicaps can understand

Family Bible Study Spanish Resources:
- *Estudios Bíblicos LifeWay™ para Adultos: Manual para el Líder*: Family Bible Study Adult Leader Guide
- *Estudios Bíblicos LifeWay™ para Adultos: Ayudas para la Enseñanza:* Family Bible Study Adult Leader Pack
- *Estudios Bíblicos LifeWay™ para Adultos: Manual para el Participante:* Family Bible Study Adult Learner Guide

Explore the Bible

Explore the Bible provides adults comprehensive studies of the books of the Bible, through systematic verse-by-verse study of all 66 Bible books. using parallel HCSB® and KJV translations.
- *Explore the Bible Adult Leader Guide:* contains commentary, leadership helps, department assembly helps, and teaching plans
- *Explore the Bible Adult Leader Pack:* contains session posters, worksheets, and a CD-ROM with leader helps
- *Explore the Bible Adult Commentary:* in-depth Bible exposition
- *Explore the Bible Adult Audiocassette:* an audio version of the Learner Guide
- *Explore the Bible Adult Learner Guide*
- *Explore the Bible Adult Learner Guide Large Print*
- *Explore the Bible Adult Study Guide*
- *Exploring the Bible: Bible Studies for the Deaf*
- *Biblical Illustrator:* use for Bible background research
- *Biblical Illustrator Plus:* quarterly CD-ROM contains the current issue of the magazine plus related articles from the archives
- *EXTRA!:* weekly online supplement to teaching plans in printed curriculum contains current events and additional teaching options, available at www.lifeway.com/myextra

Exploring the Bible Language Resources: Bible book study which has been adapted and written especially for Chinese, Vietnamese, and Korean churches.
- *Exploring the Bible: Chinese Bible Studies*
- *Exploring the Bible: Vietnamese Bible Studies*
- *Exploring the Bible: Korean Bible Studies*

MasterWork

MasterWork: Essential Messages from God's Servants is designed for adults who desire studies written by well-known and respected authors such as Billy Graham, Charles Swindoll, and Henry Blackaby.

Each quarterly study contains 13 comprehensive Bible-based sessions, using various translations of the Scripture. There are two pages of personal study per day for five weekdays and interactive learning activities for use during the session. The Leader/Learner Guide is combined into one resource.

Life Connections

Life Connections, based on the NIV translation, is designed for small group Bible study or for the master teacher approach to Sunday School. There are eight quarters of topical, nonsequential studies on Christian growth and life issues.
- *Leader Book:* contains commentary, a step-by-step guide to preparing and presenting each session, and helps for organizing the class
- *Student Book:* contains helps for daily study, multiple-choice questions for those new to the Christian community, and reference notes to help new students catch up

Adult Sunday School Leadership Resources

- *Essentials for Excellence: Connecting Sunday School to Life:* includes a CD-ROM containing helps designed specifically for Adult Sunday School leaders. It helps Adult Sunday School teachers organize a Sunday School class; develop the leaders needed for effective Adult Sunday School; and achieve excellence.
- *Leading Adults:* a 64-page quarterly magazine that examines the issues and challenges confronting leaders of adult ministry. *Leading Adults* provides practical helps and ideas for those leading Sunday School classes and departments as well as for leaders of other areas of adult ministry beyond Sunday School.

Something to Think About

Selecting Bible study curriculum is a very important decision because it impacts the long-term change that occurs through an effective Sunday School ministry. A wise curriculum selection can help facilitate a class's spiritual growth and understanding of its mission. Select studies based on a long-term direction not just short-term results.

1. If you use one of the curriculum series mentioned above, write in the margin long-term benefits it offers for effective Sunday School ministry. How does it impact the leader's growth? How does it impact the learner's growth? How does it impact the mission of the class?
2. If you don't use any of these resources, choose one that you might be interested in using. How could it impact the leader's growth? How could it impact the learner's growth? How does it impact the mission of the class?
3. Can you list some possible long-term consequences that could take place if a class did not use an ongoing curriculum plan?

   What if they chose a popular book to study, and when it was finished, they looked for another book? What would be some of the long-term consequences of this approach?

   What if the teacher or another leader wrote the lessons for each week? What could be some of the long-term consequences of this approach?

   What if the teacher decided to read passages from the Bible and then asked the group to provide insight to the passages each week? What could be some of the long-term consequences of this approach?

   What if a curriculum was chosen that was not doctrinally sound or was doctrinally unclear? What could be some long-term consequences? Fortunately, you have excellent curriculum choices, so you won't face these problems.

How To Order LifeWay Curriculum

Through your church: Each church receives a dated curriculum order form for each quarter.
By Internet: www.lifeway.com (online catalog and online dated and undated order forms)
By Telephone: 800-458-2772
By Fax: 615-251-5933
By Mail: Customer Service, MSN 113, One LifeWay Plaza, Nashville, TN 37234-0113
In Person: LifeWay Christian Stores (Life Connections only)

Additional Helpful Bible Study Tools

(From Broadman & Holman except where indicated):
Study Bibles
- *Disciple's Study Bible.* This Bible has features of both a study Bible and a life application Bible. It equips the believer for a lifetime and enables the believer to nurture other disciples along the Way.
- *Experiencing the Word New Testament–HCSB®.* This edition of the Holman Christian Standard Bible® includes Henry Blackaby's thought-provoking devotional notes.
- *KJV Master Study Bible.* The Master Study Bible has been redesigned for a new generation. The center-column reference system links you to thousands of related passages in the King James text, allowing the Bible itself to serve as it own best commentary.
- *Serendipity Interactive Study Bible,* Serendipity House, 2002. If you are teaching from the *Life Connection* resource you will find this Bible very helpful.
- *Serendipity Bible for Groups 4th Edition,* Serendipity House, 2002.

Bible Dictionaries
- *Boyd's Bible Dictionary,* by James P. Boyd. This concise, compact dictionary with thousands of Biblical references identifies all proper names, places, and events of the Scriptures, with pronunciations, definitions, and textual references.
- *The Holman Concise Bible Dictionary,* Trent C. Butler, editor, covers all the traditional topics you want in a Bible dictionary, but also has 2800 entries on contemporary topics, including abortion, AIDS, and child abuse.
- *The Holman Illustrated Bible Dictionary,* Trent C. Butler, editor, provides exhaustive definitions and articles, color photos, illustrations, charts, maps, pronunciations, and entries from seven translations.
- *Holman Treasury of Key Bible Words,* by Eugene E. Carpenter and Philip W. Comfort, offers accurate, detailed definitions of 400 key Bible words from their original Greek or Hebrew text.
- *Spanish Holman Treasury of Key Bible Words: Glosario Holman de términos bíblicos,* by Eugene E. Carpenter and Philip Wesley Comfort. The *Glosario Holman de términos bíblicos* has a clearly written explanation of 400 key Bible words.

Commentaries
Commentaries explain the meaning of Scriptures and provide background information. Consider purchasing a one-volume commentary that covers the entire

Bible. If your budget allows, consider a multivolume set that provides more detailed explanation and is more comprehensive.
- *Holman Concise Bible Commentary,* David Dockery, editor, provides a one-volume commentary on the entire Bible, designed to help the reader place the passage studied into a larger context.
- *The Teacher's Bible Commentary,* H. Franklin Paschall, Herschel H. Hobbs, editors, is a one-volume commentary, widely used by Sunday School teachers for over 25 years.
- *The New American Commentary*—multivolume.
- Holman New and Old Testament Commentaries.
- *Shepherd's Notes,* Duane A. Garrett, editor. You grew up using the well known black and yellow striped Cliff's Notes to help you grasp everything from great literary works to algebra. You'll look to these unique books for their use in Bible studies, teaching, and personal devotions.

Other Helpful Resources
- *Holman Bible Atlas,* by Thomas V. Brisco, Broadman & Holman. Full-color maps and photographs illustrate the land, sites, and archaeology of the biblical world. Information about daily life and the role of archaeology in recovering ancient cultures is discussed.
- *HCSB® Harmony of the Gospels.* This unique harmony features the four gospels woven into a single, running narrative. Hundreds of study notes illuminate the text.
- *Holman Bible Handbook,* David S. Dockery, editor. This practical tool brings an understanding of the ancient world together with the timeless message of God's Word to expand biblical insights for modern readers.
- *Holman Book of Biblical Charts, Maps, and Reconstructions.* This complete one-volume set of Bible charts, maps and artists' renderings of biblical cities and artifacts provides a deeper dimension to personal and group Bible study. Features cross-references to the Holman Bible Handbook and Holman Bible Dictionary.
- *Holman Concise Topical Concordance.* The alphabetic arrangement of topics in this concordance makes makes it easy to find key Scripture verses where a topic of interest is addressed. It's a basic tool to be found on the shelf along with the Bible itself.
- *Holman Illustrated Guide to Biblical History* by Kendell H. Easley. Photos, maps, time lines, and text all work together to help students of the Bible come to a new level of understanding about what God has done, what He does, and what He will do. Readers can see numerous connections that might otherwise have eluded them.
- *The Illustrated Life of Jesus,* by Herschel Hobbs. Hobbs weaves the gospel writers' differing perspectives into one seamless narrative, following Christ from the announcement of His birth to His glorious ascension. Includes photos, colorful graphics and sidebar information about Jesus' life and teachings.
- *Holman QuickSource Guide: Atlas of Bible Lands* packs an amazing amount of information about the physical context of biblical events in to a book that's easy to carry and easy to use.
- *Holman QuickSource Guide to Understanding the Bible* by Kendell H. Easley, is a book-by-book overview of Bible facts, background information, main idea, Christian worldview themes, major verses, and summaries of the biblical story.
- *So That's in the Bible?* John Perry, editor, contains thousands of listings on 3,700 topics, including references on contemporary issues such as abortion, rap music, capital punishment, and AIDS. Also included are more than 200 short articles that add sparkle to sermons, lessons, and group discussions.
- *That's Easy for You to Say!* by W. Murray Severance, includes the acceptable pronunciation of every proper name in every major translation of the Bible. Guidelines are based on Hebrew, Greek, and Aramaic speech. Included is a CD-ROM which enables you to hear the words first-hand.
- *Word Pictures in the New Testament*, Concise Edition, by A.T. Robertson. This classic six-volume set has been condensed into a one-volume edition.

Computer Bible Study Tools
- LifeWay's free Bible Search Tool provides commentaries, devotionals, dictionaries, word studies, seven versions of the Bible, and more. Access it at *bible.lifeway.com.* You can also reach it by clicking on "Bible Search Tool" at *www.lifeway.com.*
- Information about the new HCSB® can be found at *www.lifeway.com/lwc/.*
- *HCSB® Bible Navigator—CD,* offers powerful search features, fast cross-referencing, and an integrated word processor. This CD-ROM product includes the complete new *Holman Christian Standard Bible®,* a library of reference works, personalization features, and Internet enhancements.

CHAPTER 2

GETTING READY FOR SUNDAY'S SESSION— BEGINNING EARLY

If you truly want to guide adults toward maturity and service, you should begin early every week. Spend about 30 minutes on Sunday afternoon or Monday using the following guide to help you prepare for the next Sunday.

Evaluate the Previous Session
Before you look toward the next session, use these indicators as you examine what took place in the previous session.

(1) Bible Study
How well did you communicate the lesson? Did you provide the opportunity for decisions (salvation, recommitment, or others) to be made? How did the group respond to the lesson? In what ways did you sense God was at work? Were you able to provide specific applications of the lesson to life during the week? What can you do better next session?

_____

_____

(2) Relationships
Relationships with Each Other: Evaluate how the class interacted with each other. Were there guests? How did the class do at welcoming the guests? Were the guests registered so follow-up could take place?

Were those who attended shown appreciation? Were those absent identified, and were steps taken to contact them? Did you have someone helping you with this? What could be improved?

Relationship with God: Evaluate the prayer time. How long was it? What was the main focus of the prayer requests? Were there prayer requests for the lost? Were there updates on previous prayer requests? Did you have someone helping you with this?

_____

_____

(3) Mission
Adult class members need to understand that they are on mission when they come to Sunday School. Help them see that God's mission includes every Christian. Page 27 provides further information on the mission of a Sunday School class. How can adults develop a sense of mission?

_____

_____

Set Weekly Goals
Based on the evaluation of the previous session, set some goals in the following areas.

(1) Bible Study
What are some steps I need to take to communicate next week's lesson better?

_____

_____

(2) Relationships
- What steps need to be taken in order to follow up on guests? Who can help?

  _____

- What steps need to be taken in order to follow up with absentees? Who can help?

  _____

- Are there individuals who need encouragement or an evangelistic visit? Who can help?

  _____

- How can we best communicate the class prayer requests to all members, prospects, and members-in-service? Who can help?

  _____

- How can we help with specific prayer needs mentioned during class? Who can help?

  _____

(3) Mission
What can you do to help members understand the mission of the class? Is there biblical content in next Sunday's lesson that will provide a basis for teaching about the mission of the class? What specific actions could be taken to remind the class of their mission?

On the prayer list, are there new classes or members-in-service who need to be encouraged? Is the class preparing to start a new class? Are there evangelistic opportunities/training and discipleship events that should be emphasized?

_____

_____

Overview Next Week's Lesson
Look at the focal Bible passages and the direction of the the lesson. As you look at these items, keep the context of the entire unit of study in mind. You may want to review the unit of study every week to remind you of the context of the lesson.

An overview of the lesson begins your journey with God during the week as He teaches you how the study applies to your life.

Note to Directors of Adult Departments
Additional helps for leadership meetings are included in the PREPARE section of the *Family Bible Study* and *Explore the Bible Leader Guides*.

Practice It
These exercises help overview the next lesson by providing teachers opportunities for reflection.
For each of the four curriculum series, look at the samples provided and answer these questions:
- Which one of these elements helps you determine the focus of the lesson for the week?
- What is one thing God can teach you regarding the lesson for the week?
- What do you think God wants to teach your class through this lesson?

Sample 1
Explore the Bible

Week of December 7

RESPONDING TO GOD'S CALL

Background Passage: Jonah 1:1–2:9
Lesson Passages: Jonah 1:1-12,17; 2:1-2

BIBLICAL SETTING
1. Jonah's Rebellion (Jonah 1:1-3)
2. God's Discipline (Jonah 1:4-17)
3. Jonah's Repentance (Jonah 2:1-9)

LESSON PASSAGES OUTLINE
1. Refusing God's Leadership (Jonah 1:1-3)
2. Experiencing God's Discipline (Jonah 1:4-12,17)
3. Submitting to God (Jonah 2:1-2)

KEY BIBLE VERSES
Jonah 2:8-9

BIBLICAL TRUTH
God expects His people to follow His leadership to share His truth with all people.

LIFE IMPACT
To help you follow God's leadership in helping to share His truth with people who need to hear it and respond to it

For **Explore the Bible:** Look at Sample 1 on this page or turn to the beginning of a lesson in your own *Leader Guide*. Locate and read the following.

- Study Theme Introduction (Find page number in your *Leader Guide* table of contents. No sample provided.)
- Background Passage
- Key Bible Verse
- Lesson Passage
- Biblical Truth
- Biblical Setting
- Life Impact
- Lesson Passage Outline
- Session Goal (not shown on this sample)

For **Family Bible Study:** Look at Sample 2 on this page or turn to the beginning of a lesson in your own *Leader Guide*. Locate and consider the following.

- Study Theme Introduction (Find page number in your *Leader Guide* table of contents. No sample provided.)
- Life Question
- Bible Passage
- Scripture Outline
- Biblical Setting
- Biblical Truth
- Key Bible Verse
- Life Impact
- Session Goal (not shown)

Sample 2
Family Bible Study

Week of January 4

God Chooses and Equips

Life Question
How can I know God can use me?

BIBLE PASSAGE: 1 Samuel 16:1-13

SCRIPTURE OUTLINE
God Is Sovereign (1 Sam. 16:1-3)
God Has His Own Standards (1 Sam. 16:4-10)
God Uses the Unlikely (1 Sam. 16:11-13)

BIBLICAL SETTING
The prophet Samuel had anointed Saul as Israel's first king (1 Sam. 9:15–10:1). Because of disobedience on Saul's part, God eventually rejected Saul as king over Israel. God instructed Samuel to go to the house of Jesse in Bethlehem, where Samuel would anoint one of Jesse's sons as Israel's new king.

BIBLICAL TRUTH
In choosing and equipping believers to accomplish His work in the world, God places priority on the heart.

KEY BIBLE VERSE
1 Samuel 16:7

LIFE IMPACT
To help you live in readiness to be used by God in whatever ways He desires

PREPARE

10

For **MasterWork:** Look at Samples 3 and 4 on this page, or turn to the beginning of lesson in your own book. Locate and consider the following:
- Book Introduction (Find page number in your *Leader/Learner Guide* table of contents or see Sample 3.)
- Day One of the week's study
- Briefly look over the titles and focus of each day's study during the week in your own book.

Sample 3
MasterWork

Walking Wisely

It's one thing to start out on a path God calls you to follow. It's another thing to continue to walk on that path day in and day out, year in and year out, for a lifetime.

It's one thing to accept Jesus Christ and to experience the exuberance of knowing that your sins are forgiven, you have been filled with God's Holy Spirit, and you are called into a newness of life. It's another thing to walk the Christian life in wisdom month after month, problem after problem, difficulty after difficulty.

Many voices will call to you to lure you away from God's wise path. You must say "no" to those voices, even when the allure is powerful, the temptation is strong, the rewards seem bright, or the detour seems easy.

Walk wisely! Stay on the path! Get God's viewpoint. Do what the Word of God tells you to do. Follow the promptings of the Holy Spirit. Determine in your heart that you will choose God's way over your own way. Determine in your heart that you will trust God day by day. And you will walk in wisdom . . . all the way to eternity's door.

GETTY IMAGES

Charles STANLEY

Earthly Wisdom vs. Godly Wisdom

day One

Only Two Ways to Walk

There are only two ways to walk in this life—wisely or unwisely. There are only two types of choices—wise or unwise. Throughout the Scriptures God admonishes His people to walk wisely.

As you read what God's Word boldly declares about wisdom, underline the dividends of wisdom. Circle the benefit that most appeals to you.

> Happy is the man who finds wisdom,
> And the man who gains understanding;
> For her proceeds are better than the profits of silver,
> And her gain than fine gold.
> She is more precious than rubies,
> And all the things you may desire cannot compare with her.
> Length of days is in her right hand,
> In her left hand riches and honor.
> Her ways are ways of pleasantness,
> And all her paths are peace.
> She is a tree of life to those who take hold of her,
> And happy are all who retain her. (Proverbs 3:13-18)

Wisdom is the capacity to see things from God's perspective and to respond to them according to scriptural principles. In other words, wisdom is seeking heavenly opinions on earthly circumstances.

Sample 4
MasterWork

For Life Connections: Look at Samples 5 and 6 on this page, or turn to the beginning of the lesson in your own *Leader Book*. Locate and consider the following:
- Goals for Bible Study (located on page 2 of lesson)
- Goals for Life Change (located on page 2 of lesson)
- Read ". . . about today's session"
- Read the focal passages for the week (located on page 3 of lesson).

**Sample 5
Life Connections**

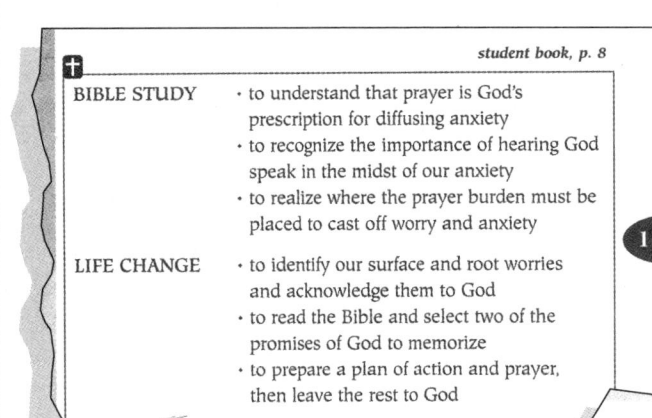

student book, p. 8

BIBLE STUDY
- to understand that prayer is God's prescription for diffusing anxiety
- to recognize the importance of hearing God speak in the midst of our anxiety
- to realize where the prayer burden must be placed to cast off worry and anxiety

LIFE CHANGE
- to identify our surface and root worries and acknowledge them to God
- to read the Bible and select two of the promises of God to memorize
- to prepare a plan of action and prayer, then leave the rest to God

**Sample 6
Life Connections**

...about today's session (5 minutes)

AN ANTIDOTE FOR ANXIETY

The author of *Don't Sweat the Small Stuff* tapped into the national panic regarding the seemingly all-consuming stress of everyday life. With all our technological advances, we are discovering that the evil twin of rapid development may be rampant anxiety. Therapists are not only treating thousands of adults with anxiety disorders but they are also treating anxiety in young children, most from financially secure homes who are demonstrating symptoms not even seen in children from war-torn nations!

As adults, we face issues regarding career, finances, marriage, children, aging parents, health, and schedule overload—just to name a few. Into that chaos we hear the apostle Paul say, "Do not be anxious about anything" (Phil. 4:6), and something inside us wants to retort, "Get real, buddy!" The subtitle of *Don't Sweat the Small Stuff* is *And It's All Small Stuff*. But when your 80-year-old mother who lives 300 miles away has fallen and broken her hip, it's not small stuff. When your husband is laid off, it's not small stuff. When your daughter is separating from her husband, it's not small stuff. And when all that is happening simultaneously, it's definitely not small stuff!

Paul's therapeutic counsel for anxiety would hardly be credible if not for the fact that he models the treatment plan and demonstrates its success. Remember, Paul is in prison facing possible execution. When a man is inching his way toward death row and says, "You don't have to be a prisoner of worry," it makes you want to hear him out. In today's session, we'll study the words of our incarcerated counselor.

CHAPTER 3

GETTING READY FOR SUNDAY'S SESSION—STUDYING THE LESSON

I teach an Adult Sunday School class every Sunday. However, I don't prepare my lesson until Friday night or Saturday. Now don't jump to conclusions. I do prepare my heart throughout the week.

Letting God teach us is vital preparation for an effective lesson on Sunday. We must allow time for Him to teach us how the lesson applies to our own lives personally. My goal is never to go to class on Sunday without God having already changed my life through the Bible study during the week.

If I prepare my heart adequately, the lesson that I prepare for Sunday not only becomes easier to prepare but becomes more meaningful because God has already used it to change my life. Even though I don't prepare the lesson until the end of the week, I do prepare myself—I just focus on my heart first!

Prepare Your Heart Daily

In the days following your initial evaluation, goal setting, and content review, use the following ideas as a guide. Remember, this is only a devotional study at this point. Give God time to teach you. If you follow these steps, you can spend about 15–30 minutes per day preparing your heart. As this takes place, God also begins to teach you how to present the lesson on Sunday.

- *Break the study down into daily increments.* Look at the *Leader Guide* passages and commentary and determine how it can be broken down into daily segments of study.
- *Read the Bible passages devotionally.* Read the passage several times, noting words or phrases you do not completely understand and concepts you want to explore later. Meditate on the passage.
- *Read the Bible passages analytically.* Read the Scripture in more than one translation. Use a Bible dictionary to look up unfamiliar words. Write down questions that come to mind. Make notes about new insights you're gaining from meditating on God's Word. Look up parallel passages in your study Bible.
- *Reflect on the Bible's message and application.* Ask yourself: What does the Bible say? What does the passage mean? What does it mean for me and my class members? What should I think, feel, or do as a result of this Scripture?
- *Study the commentary provided.* Each LifeWay resource provides commentary that relates to the Scripture passages being studied.
- *Answer any questions* related to the passages that the daily study might provide.
- *Daily review prayer lists from Sunday and the goals you set for the week related to relationships and mission.* Determine if there is some action that needs to be taken and who can help you.
- *Spend time in prayer* regarding what God is teaching you as well as for other needs related to you and your class.

Use Additional Resources to Gain Deeper Understanding

A variety of supplemental resources can help answer questions that might arise while you are studying the Scriptures. Consider using some of the additional resources listed in chapter 1 to enhance your Bible study time.

Practice It

Practice the steps in "Prepare Your Heart Daily" using the curriculum samples that follow on pages 14–16 or the Leader Guide in the curriculum you currently use.

For **Family Bible Study:** Look at the *Leader Guide* you are currently using or look at Samples 7 and 8 on this page and mark items that relate to the steps listed on page 13. Then practice the steps by using the items you identified.

**Samples 7 & 8
Family Bible Study**

WEEK OF FEBRUARY 1

DISCIPLINED WORSHIP

LIFE QUESTION

Why do I need to worship regularly?

BACKGROUND PASSAGE: Psalm 95:1-11; Hebrews 10:19-25
FOCAL PASSAGE: Psalm 95:1-7a; Hebrews 10:19-25

SCRIPTURE OUTLINE
Respond to the Invitation (Ps. 95:1-2)
Focus on God (Ps. 95:3-7a)
Draw Near to God (Heb. 10:19-23)
Fulfill Church Responsibilities (Heb. 10:24-25)

**PREPARE
(CONTINUED)**

Spiritual Preparation Through Personal Bible Study

The small groups of people seemed intent in their worship. Some knelt before an image drawn on the wall. Others stood with heads bowed while making curious signs before a statue. A few were throwing butter at a massive, strange-looking stone creature. My interpreter in this eastern country explained that the first group was praying to the image, the second was trying to cancel out the "bad luck" of the idol, while the third was trying to use the butter to "cool down" the anger of the stone giant.

I could not help but think about the millions of people back in my homeland who have the truth of God's Word rather than the lies of superstition, the living Lord rather than a stone idol, and the freedom to worship the true God in thousands of churches across our nation. Yet sadly, many professing Christians neglect the great privilege of praising and worshiping the Almighty God. Worship services commonly have such low priority in people's lives that they use any excuse for not attending. Among those who do attend, many merely go through the motions and do not truly worship. In addition, countless believers spend little or no time in private worship during the week. Nevertheless, God expects His people to worship Him. Practicing the discipline of worship, both personal and corporate, is vital as a means of growing in Christlikeness. Let the truth of the Scriptures in this week's Bible study lead you to a fresh commitment to practice the discipline of worship.

Respond to the Invitation
(Ps. 95:1-2)

¹**O come, let us sing unto the LORD: let us make a joyful noise to the rock of our salvation.**
²**Let us come before his presence with thanksgiving, and make a joyful noise unto him with psalms.**

Verse 1. In some religions, worship is a coerced activity. Either by cultural customs or by laws enforced by religious authorities, multitudes participate in worship activities out of fear. They do not experience the joy that characterizes genuine and willing worship of the Lord. Rather, they steal glances at those who may be watching them, worried that they might incur the wrath of religious leaders or the "gods" whom they are worshiping.

The Lord God does not force anyone to worship Him; instead, He invites us to worship Him. The psalmist expre

For **Explore the Bible:** Look at the *Leader Guide* you are currently using or look at Samples 9 and 10 on this page and mark items that relate to the steps listed on page 13. Then practice the steps by using the items you identified.

Week *of* December 7

RESPONDING TO GOD'S CALL

Background Passage: Jonah 1:1–2:9
Lesson Passages: Jonah 1:1-12,17; 2:1-2

BIBLICAL SETTING
1. Jonah's Rebellion (Jonah 1:1-3)
2. God's Discipline (Jonah 1:4-17)
3. Jonah's Repentance (Jonah 2:1-9)

Samples 9 & 10
Explore the Bible

PREPARE
(continued)

Personal Bible Study for the Teacher

Have you ever received a sign from God? Has God ever directly given you a message about what He wants you to do? A few years ago billboards in some cities had humorous yet serious messages from God. People often smiled at the idea of God communicating with us through ordinary road signs. Some people today, even some who believe that God exists, reject as absurd the idea that God wants to communicate with human beings.

Christians, however, know that God is real and that He communicates with us today. He speaks to us primarily through His written Word, the Bible. We also communicate with Him through prayer. Christians believe that God wants all people to know Him and that God wants to communicate through believers the good news about the salvation He has provided in Christ. Some believers, however, are reluctant to obey God in sharing His truth with people who need to hear it and respond to it.

Are you consistently sharing the good news of the salvation God has provided with lost people around you? Why or why not?

Three of the four lessons this month focus on Jonah's life. Although Jonah resisted God's leadership in his life, we can learn some positive lessons from his rebellious example. Studying these Bible passages can challenge you and learners in your class to a deeper understanding of God's missionary mandate for all believers. These lessons can help you experience the **Life Impact** of following God's leadership in helping to share His truth with people who need to hear it and respond to it.

As you continue your personal Bible study, prayerfully read the **Background Passage** and respond to the **Study Questions** as well as to the questions in the margins for the December 7 lesson in *Explore the Bible: Adult Learner Guide.*

THE BIBLE IN CONTEXT (JONAH 1:1-2:9)

The Book of Jonah is part of the section of the Old Testament called the Minor Prophets. The events in the Book of Jonah occurred in the eighth century B.C. (see 2 Kings 14:25). Much of the story took place outside of Israel.

The Book of Jonah begins with the Lord's commanding Jonah to go to Nineveh to preach against its wickedness. Jonah disobeyed God and boarded a ship headed to Tarshish. God caused a storm to afflict the ship's crew

For **MasterWork:** Look at Sample 11 on this page, or use your own copy of MasterWork. Look at the daily assignments for an upcoming lesson and mark items that relate to the steps mentioned on page 13. Then practice the steps by using the items you identified.

For **Life Connections:** Look at Sample 12 on this page, or use the *Leader Book* and mark items that relate to the steps mentioned on page 13. Then practice the steps by using the items you identified.

**Sample 11
MasterWork**

Beth MOORE

day two

Counselor

The Hebrew word for "Counselor" is *ya'ats*. The word encompasses many of the meanings you might expect: advising, counseling, admonishing, directing. It also involves the activity of devising plans toward certain purposes. By virtue of my calling, I am often asked by a seeking, hurting woman, "Do you think I need counseling to get over this?" My response has become, "Yes, absolutely, you need counseling every single day. So do I, and so does every single believer on earth."

Whether or not God purposes for that counsel to temporarily take place through a godly human vessel, we all require ongoing counsel in order to receive specific direction from the Lord. God desires that we make and keep our appointments for counseling so He can advise us in the matters of daily living.

Read the definition of counselor again. As you consider the elements of the definition, it might be helpful to think of the counsel of God this way: The purpose of God's counsel is to make His plan for your life your own.

Look up the following Scripture verses. Identify what each tells you about the plan of God for your life.

Ephesians 1:11 _____

Psalm 33:11 _____

Proverbs 16:9 _____

Proverbs 19:21 _____

Jeremiah 29:11 _____

**Sample 12
Life Connections**

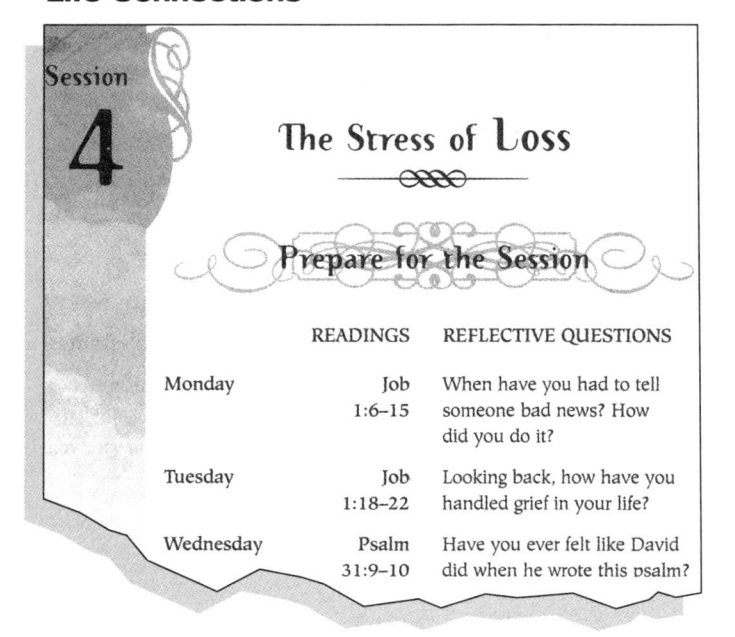

Session 4

The Stress of Loss

Prepare for the Session

	READINGS	REFLECTIVE QUESTIONS
Monday	Job 1:6–15	When have you had to tell someone bad news? How did you do it?
Tuesday	Job 1:18–22	Looking back, how have you handled grief in your life?
Wednesday	Psalm 31:9–10	Have you ever felt like David did when he wrote this psalm?

CHAPTER 4

GETTING READY FOR SUNDAY'S SESSION—CRAFTING AN EFFECTIVE LESSON

Now that you have spent several days allowing God to teach you the lesson, it is time to begin preparing the teaching plan for Sunday. An effective teaching plan can lead to a breakthrough experience for learners in your class. If you have adequately prepared during the week, it should only take you about one to two hours to finish the process. There are two keys to lesson planning you need to remember.

Key #1: Plan with the end in mind. Know your target for the session. This really takes you back to chapter two in this book where we discussed how to overview the lesson. By now, you already know the direction the lesson should go. That enables you to carry out Key #2.

Key #2: Customize! Only you and God know exactly what your members need. You know their needs, and you know the methods that best help them learn. You have been praying for them during the week. God has been speaking to you about the lesson, and He has been preparing the hearts of your learners as well.

The suggested teaching plans in any curriculum are beginning points for you in crafting an effective lesson. But they won't be effective without a prepared teacher. You must take the teaching plans and procedures and—with God's guidance—customize the lesson for your situation.

Seven Steps to Customizing the Lesson
The seven steps to customizing a lesson can easily be applied to any LifeWay adult curriculum or to the Access Leader Guide for adults who have special needs. (Additional helps for preparing to teach all adults, including those with special needs, are found on the CD-ROM within *Essentials for Excellence: Connecting Sunday School to Life,* by Louis Hanks and Alan Raughton.)

Step One: *Read completely through the suggested teaching procedures.* Most *Leader Guides* provide a step-by-step teaching plan. Read through each step and take note of the procedures that will work with your class. Note procedures that you know won't work. Place a question mark beside procedures that might work. Write down any ideas you might have regarding alternate procedures.

Practice It
Answer the following questions as you work with samples from the curriculum series on pages 18-20.
- What is one procedure you know would work and why?
- What is one procedure you don't think will work and why?
- What is one procedure you aren't sure about? How could you modify it to make it more effective?

For Family Bible Study, Explore the Bible, and MasterWork: Locate and review the material indicated for your curriculum on Sample 13, 14, 15, or 16, pages 18–20. Then answer the "Practice It" questions on page 17.

Sample 13 Family Bible Study

ENCOUNTER

A teaching plan for use with Life Answers Learner Guide
Adaptable for use with Christian Single Plus

How Should I Give?

LIFE QUESTION: How can I best honor God in my giving?

SESSION GOAL: To help adults understand the kind of giving that honors God and evaluate their own attitudes toward giving

BUILD RELATIONSHIPS AND CREATE READINESS FOR BIBLE STUDY

Teaching Notes and Learning Activities

- Learner guides
- Pens or pencils
- Giving and Receiving Poster (Pack Item 1)

Pie chart ... (learner guide, p. 19)

1 INTRODUCTION

Display the **Giving and Receiving Poster** (Pack Item 1). As learners arrive, encourage them to complete the activity on page 18 of the learner guide. Create a chart on the board and survey the class to see how many believe each statement is from the Bible. Correct responses to the questions are at the bottom of page 29 in this leader guide.

Point out that "God loves a cheerful giver" is found in 2 Corinthians 9:7. Call attention to the **Giving and Receiving Poster** (Pack Item 1) and read aloud the title of today's lesson. Ask a learner to read aloud the question at the top of page 18 in the learner guide (*If I'm giving, does my attitude really matter?*). Read aloud the quote at the top of page 19 in the learner guide. Ask a volunteer to share a brief testimony about a personal characteristic he or she learned from his or her parents. Direct learners to consider the pie chart at the bottom of page 19 in the learner guide and to circle the statement that best represents their attitudes toward giving.

EXAMINE AND APPLY GOD'S WORD

What might be the consequences ... (learner guide, p. 19)

- Consequences Poster (Pack Item 3)

Find *EXTRA!* help online at http://www.lifeway.com/extra

2 GIVE EAGERLY (2 COR. 9:1-5)

Enlist a volunteer to read aloud 1 Corinthians 9:1-5. Ask learners to suggest some responses to the activity on page 20 in the learner guide. Discuss responses. Ask: *What makes paying someone's rent a priority?* Discuss responses. Ask: *What causes people to not make giving to God a priority?* Discuss responses.

Display the **Consequences Poster** (Pack Item 3). Ask learners to discuss the simple truth represented by the words "sin, consequences, questions." Use the poster to help explain a situation from the questions back through the consequences, to the sin. Be careful not to suggest that every negative circumstance is the result of sin. However, do help learners understand that obedience in all areas, including money, keeps one in a right relationship with God.

Discussion Option: *What are some things you are eager to do? What makes you eager about one thing and not so eager about something else? What caused the Corinthians to be eager to give? What keeps you from being eager to give?*

30 LIFE ANSWERS LEADER GUIDE

**Sample 15
MasterWork**

Charles STANLEY

leader Guide

Before the Session
1. Bring the index cards participants gave you last week with prayer requests for guidance.
2. Prepare three group assignment sheets using the questions below in Step 7 of "During the Session."

During the Session
1. Welcome participants. Open with prayer requests and prayer.
2. Review the eight benefits of wisdom from last week's lesson. Ask volunteers to share how they received guidance in a circumstance this week. If that guidance was a specific answer to the request they identified on a card last week, write how and when God answered that prayer on the card. Return it to the participant as a reminder of how God answered that prayer.
3. Read aloud Essential #1 for walking wisely. Ask someone to read Proverbs 2:1-7. Request participants state verbs from this passage that demonstrate diligence in seeking wisdom. Ask: *Do most Christians apply more effort toward acquiring wealth or wisdom? What needs to change in our lives so we desire God's wisdom more than wealth?*
4. Invite someone to read aloud Essential #2. Ask participants to complete the activity on Proverbs 11:2 and share their responses.
5. Ask a volunteer to read James 1:5-8. Ask: *Why is a doubter compared to a wave of the sea? Identify specific "winds" that toss us around when we lack faith. How do these verses encourage us to ask for wisdom with complete faith?*
6. State Essential #3. Ask someone to read Psalm 119:97. Ask: *What does it mean to meditate on God's Word?*
7. Organize the class into three groups. Distribute an assignment sheet to each group.

Assignment for Group 1: Read Psalm 119:98-100. (1.) Was the psalmist bragging about himself? Explain your answer. (2.) What statements in these verses explain why the psalmist had greater wisdom than wise men? (3.) Can a person read and know God's Word and still not be wise? Why?

**Sample 14
Explore the Bible**

ENCOUNTER
(continued)

**Step 3
Key to Knowledge
(Prov. 1:7)**
 Use the *Exploration* feature on page 60 to explain the term "Fear of the Lord."
 Read aloud Proverbs 1:7. Suggest one of the following situations to individual (or pairs of) learners: *dealing with a strong-willed child; coping with a long-term illness; deciding about a job change; dealing with the death of a loved one; deciding whether to retire.* (You may substitute other situations appropriate for your class.)
 Ask: *How can the fear of the Lord be the key to knowledge in this situation?* Call for learners to share their responses.

**Step 4
Admonition of Love
(Prov. 1:8-9)**
 In advance cut yellow construction paper into strips about an inch wide.
 Read aloud Proverbs 1:8-9. Give each learner a strip of yellow paper and a pencil. Instruct individual learners to write on one side of the strip the best advice their parents ever gave them and on the other side the wisdom they most want to pass on to their children.
 Call for volunteers to share their responses. After each

ADMONITI
HCSB

8 Listen, my son, to your father's in
and don't reject your mother's teaching,
9 for they will be a garland of grace on yo
and a ⌊gold⌋ chain around your neck.

58 *Way of Wisdom*

**Sample 16
MasterWork**

Week of JANUARY 18

Assignment for Group 2: Read Psalm 119:101-104. (1.) What kept the psalmist from evil? (2.) What's the relationship between a love for God's Word and right living? (3.) Can a person read and know God's Word and still choose the wrong way to live? Why?

Assignment for Group 3: Read Psalm 119:105. (1.) What object did the psalmist use to illustrate the role God's Word played in his life? (2.) Why did he choose that object? (3.) What object would you have chosen? Why? (4.) Can people read and know God's Word and still be in the dark? Why?

8. Allow groups several moments to complete their assignment. Request they share their responses.
9. Ask a volunteer to read Essential #4. As a group, complete the activity related to the two-pronged process of meditating on God's Word. Ask: *To which of the two prongs do you think most Christians pay attention? Why? How can we learn to treasure God's commands?*
10. Read Essential #5. Ask volunteers to read aloud the Scripture passages related to the Holy Spirit's promptings. Determine together which actions best describe the Spirit's promptings in each passage. Allow volunteers to share how they have experienced the Spirit's prompting and how they responded. Share a personal experience to start the discussion.
11. Read aloud Essential #6. Ask participants to name their favorite places or objects of God's creation. Ask, *How do these elements of God's creation help us to be wise about God's ways?*
12. Read Essential #7. Ask learners to share how a wise person has influenced them. Guide the class to discuss specific ways they can be wise influences on young persons in your church and community.
13. Use the final activity in the column on page 89 to review the seven essentials for walking wisely. Allow volunteers to share which essentials may have been a new thought to them and why.
14. Intr...

For **Life Connections,** locate the section that begins with the title, "Icebreaker," Sample 17 and 18, pages 20 and 21. Review the lesson from there until the end. Then answer the questions under "Practice It" on page 17.

INTRODUCE THE ICEBREAKER ACTIVITY: The students have been given instructions in their books.

After the Icebreaker say something like, "Sports bloopers make everyone laugh—everyone except the blooper maker. Sometimes our mistakes have minimal impact and we can laugh about them later. Sometimes the consequences are far-reaching and prompt no laughter. Today we'll examine the story of Peter, a fighter who pridefully vowed to go the distance against any enemy, then was knocked out after only three rounds."

will give us en...gement a... to minimize future failures

Icebreaker (10-15 minutes)

Penalties, Turnovers, and Bloopers. Which of the following best describes one of your recent mistakes?

☐ FUMBLE—I was taking a lot of hits and eventually I messed up.
☐ CENTER FIELD COLLISION—I think I may have hurt someone on my team.
☐ OFFSIDES—I responded hastily.
☐ TECHNICAL FOUL—I said something I should not have said.
☐ DELAY OF GAME—I didn't plan my time very well and didn't get the job done.
☐ HOLE IN MY GLOVE—I don't know how it happened.
☐ BLOWN LAY-UP—I must have lost concentration.
☐ Other: _____

notes:

**Sample 17
Life Connections**

**Sample 18
Life Connections**

LEARNING FROM THE BIBLE

MATTHEW 26:31-35

Have a member of the class, selected ahead of time, read the passages from Matthew.

MATTHEW 26:69-75

Summarize these introductory remarks. Be sure to include the underlined information, which gives the answers to the student book questions (provided in the margin).

---

student book, pp. 17-18

Bible Study (30-45 minutes)

The Scripture for this week:

³¹Jesus told them, "This very night you will all fall away on account of me, for it is written:

"'I will strike the shepherd,
   and the sheep of the flock will be scattered.'

³²But after I have risen, I will go ahead of you into Galilee." ³³Peter replied, "Even if all fall away on account of you, I never will." ³⁴"I tell you the truth," Jesus answered, "this very night, before the rooster crows, you will disown me three times." ³⁵But Peter declared, "Even if I have to die with you, I will never disown you." And all the other disciples said the same. ...

⁶⁹Peter was sitting out in the courtyard, and a servant girl came to him. "You also were with Jesus of Galilee," she said. ⁷⁰But he denied it before them all. "I don't know what you're talking about," he said.
⁷¹Then he went out to the gateway, where another girl saw him and said to the people there, "This fellow was with Jesus of Nazareth." ⁷²He denied it again, with an oath: "I don't know the man!"
⁷³After a little while, those standing there went up to Peter and said, "Surely you are one of them, for your accent gives you away."
⁷⁴Then he began to call down curses on himself and he swore to them, "I don't know the man!"
Immediately a rooster crowed. ⁷⁵Then Peter remembered the word Jesus had spoken: "Before the rooster crows, you will disown me three times." And he went outside and wept bitterly.

...about today's session (5 minutes)

LESSONS FROM LOSS

Golf is a very unforgiving game. Leave the club face open just a little too much and you'll slice the ball so far into the woods it will take a search party to find it. While golf itself is not very forgiving, recreational golfers are always seeking and granting themselves mercy. For example, instead of taking a two-stroke penalty for hitting the ball into the water (isn't losing an expensive golf ball penalty enough?) the duffer will turn to his snickering but understanding partners and request a "mulligan," which is a golf term for a do-over or second chance.

20

Step Two: *Review available* **Leader Pack** *resources.* (Available with *Family Bible Study* and *Explore the Bible*) Leader Packs contain items such as posters, maps, and additional activities. Look through the items provided and determine which you could use to enhance your learning environment.

Step Three: *Review the CD-ROM in the available* **Leader Packs.** (Available with *Family Bible Study* and *Explore the Bible*) The CD-ROM is a vital part of your customization process. It contains the commentary and teaching plans for the Family Bible Study or Explore the Bible curriculum. You can use your computer's word processing program to create a custom document with the provided commentary and teaching procedures you've chosen from the CD-ROM. You can also insert your own comments and procedures.

If you use the CD-ROM, you can develop a teaching plan that is no more than four half pages long which will fit inside your Bible. Then the focus of the lesson remains on the Bible and not on a *Leader Guide* that you have to refer to repeatedly. The CD-ROM helps you customize your lesson and leave the *Leader Guide* at home.

Step Four: *Review additional teaching resources:*
• Review *EXTRA!* and other online resources at *www.lifeway.com*.
• Review items provided in *QuickSource*. *QuickSource* is to teaching plans what Hobbs is to commentary. It provides two additional one-page teaching plans for each lesson, one built around a discussion approach and the other around an object lesson, along with ideas suitable for specific audiences.

Step Five: *Review the* **Learner Guide.** The *Learner Guide* is the most valuable tool the teacher has. It assures that the lesson doesn't end with the session, and it also provides activities that can be used during the session. The *Learner Guide* is not only a tool for the teacher but also a resource for the learner. Therefore, you should teach learners how to use it and help them see the value of it.

Determine how the *Learner Guide* content may be used during the class and how it can help continue the Bible study following the session. Teach learners how to use the *Learner Guide* by using at least one *Learner Guide* activity during the session and by suggesting at least one activity to use during the week following the session.

Practice It
Review your *Learner Guide* and mark one item or activity that you feel would work very well during the class session. The item may or may not have been included in the teaching procedures. Why do you feel that it would work?

Review your *Learner Guide* and mark one item or activity that you feel would work well after the session as a follow-up activity. The item may or may not have been included in the teaching procedures. Why do you feel that it would work with your class?

Step Six: *Determine ways to apply the lesson following the session.*
Remember that the lesson doesn't end when the session does. It should continue into the week following the session.

Practice It
For Explore the Bible *and* Family Bible Study:
- Review CONTINUE in the *Leader Guide* or on this page, Sample 19, to determine a plan of action for leading the group to continue Bible study, ministry, evangelism, and fellowship.

- Point out the daily follow-up or preparation activities in the *Learner Guide* each week.
- If *Learner Guides* are not available, determine ways to conclude each session with at least one suggestion for using the lesson during the week.

For MasterWork:
- Review "After the Session" in the *Leader Guide* section of each study or in Sample 20 on this page.

Sample 20
MasterWork

tials may have been a new thought to them and why.
14. Introduce a time of silent prayer by asking adults to prayerfully choose one or two essentials they will begin to work on this week. After a few moments, close in prayer.

After the Session
1. Contact recent absentees. Tell them what you have enjoyed about this study on walking wisely and encourage them to attend next week.
2. Write a card to someone you consider wise. Thank the person for the godly influence he or she has had on your life.
3. Read next week's content and complete the learning activities. Follow the suggestions in "Before the Session."

Sample 19
Explore the Bible and Family Bible Study

CONTINUE
BIBLE STUDY AND MINISTRY

1. Set an example for learners by using "Learning and Living the Bible Lesson" (see p. 93 in the learner guide) as a devotional guide to prepare next week's lesson.
2. Get with others in your family or among your friends to follow the suggestion in "Family Bible Time" (p. 92 in the learner guide). Use this as a time to consider new ways you could embrace life's value this week.
3. Be sure to read the article "Being a Pro-Life Christian" (pp. 86-87). Chose something definite you will do to affirm the sanctity of human life this week. Perhaps some member of your class has a special need you can meet. Maybe you can get members to join you in a group project.
4. Write notes of encouragement to guests or call to invite them to join your class again for Bible Study.

[1]Donald S. Whitney, *Spiritual Disciplines of the Christian Life* (Colorado Springs: NavPress, 1991), 44.

For **Life Connections***:*
• Review the Life Change Lessons in the Leader and Student books or in Sample 21 on this page.

Sample 21
Life Connections

> ### life change lessons (5-7 minutes)
>
> The old saying is, "To have a friend you've got to be one." The idea behind this saying is that if we are self-focused, concerned about what we do or do not have in terms of friendship, then we won't be considering the acts of friendship that *others* need. As a result, they'll have no reason to be our friend. It's very similar to something that Jesus said, "For whoever wants to save his life will lose it" (Matt. 16:25). So as we seek to apply this week's session, we need to look at some specific things we can do to be real friends to others. Here are some suggestions that are in line with what we have been talking about:
>
> 1. SET ASIDE AT LEAST THREE HOURS THIS COMING WEEK FOR FRIENDSHIP BUILDING. This time could be used for calling people to see how they are doing, for having a cup of coffee with someone, for helping someone with a project, or whatever fits your mutual interests.
>
> 2. SHARE SOMETHING NEW ABOUT YOURSELF WITH A FRIEND. Think through what it is that you want to share ahead of time. It should reveal something significant about you. The person you choose to share this with should be someone you are willing to trust and who you want to know better.
>
> 3. IDENTIFY AT LEAST TWO TALENTS A FRIEND HAS AND ENCOURAGE HIM OR HER IN AT LEAST ONE OF THEM. Encouraging a friend can mean anything from complimenting how you've seen him or her use a talent, to attending an event (concert, game, worship service, class, etc.) where your friend is using that talent and giving positive feedback about what you experience.
>
> 15

Step Seven: *Develop an outline of your session*
Prepare a Sunday School session that's 45 to 60 minutes in length (depending on your church's schedule). The plan should follow a logical flow. Consider the following steps to organize your session:

• ***Build Relationships and Focus on Mission.*** Relationship building provides continuity from week-to-week and provides the maximum opportunity for learning to take place. Provide a time in which learners can fellowship, greet each other and guests, and pray together.

Emphasize the class mission. Prayer for members, new class starts, the lost, and for the ministry needs of the class to take place. Make announcements regarding church and class events. Discuss weekly ministry actions such as visitation, absentee contacts, and ministry needs that have surfaced.

If the beginning of class is not an appropriate time, consider doing this at the end of the session. It helps the learner put the lesson into focus.

• ***Introduction.*** The lesson introduction motivates learners by creating an interest in the Bible study. It helps adults recognize how the biblical truth will answer a life question or meet a life need.

• ***Examine and apply the Scripture.*** The heart of the lesson leads learners to discover the answers to several basic questions. *What does the Scripture say? What does it mean? What does it mean to me?*

• ***Encourage life change based on the Biblical Truth.*** The lesson should end with learners answering the question: *What should I think, feel, or do as a result of understanding this Scripture?*

• ***Continue the lesson and ministry.*** Develop a plan that leads learners to apply the lesson through the ministry of the Sunday School class. Usually this is implemented after the session concludes.

The plan sheet on page 24 can assist you as you customize your lesson.

Additional resources for teachers of special needs classes The CD-ROM in the back of the Essentials for Excellence book (see page 17 for description) contains valuable helps: an e-book; articles; forms; handouts; PowerPoint® visuals; a teaching plan; and teaching resources.

Sunday School Session Plan Sheet

Title _____

Session Goal _____

Build Relationships

- Welcome guests and affirm those in attendance.
- Make any announcements regarding church or class events.
- Discuss weekly ministry actions (visitation, absentee contacts, ministry needs, and so forth)
- Pray for the lost, new class starts, members-in-service, and other class needs.
- List prayer concerns on the back of this sheet.

Bible Study

Lesson Introduction

Items needed

Examine and Apply God's Word *(Provide a step-by-step plan)*

Conclusion—Encourage Life Change

Continue the Lesson and Ministry

Sunday School Session Plan Sheet. © Copyright 2003. LifeWay Christian Resources of the Southern Baptist Convention. All rights reserved.
NOTE: Permission is granted by the copyright holder to make photocopies of this item for its intended use only.

CHAPTER 5

EXPERIENCING GOD DURING THE SESSION

You have prayed, studied, and prepared to teach for change, and it is time for Sunday School. Cover these basics to make your Sunday session work smoothly.

Arrive Early
Arrive early enough to set up the room and to prepare the focal wall. Teachers should arrive at least 15 minutes before the scheduled time for the session. It is hard to come in late, set up, and still establish rapport with those who are in the room. Arriving late can sidetrack all you have planned and prepared for during the week.

Set Up the Room
Focal wall and the learning environment
- Make sure that everything on the focal wall points to the lesson that is being taught. Announcements, pictures, or bulletins should be placed on a bulletin board somewhere away from the focal wall. A good place for announcements is near the entrance to the room or near a coffee pot if you have one in the room.
- Place something on the focal wall—a poster, a question on the board, an outline, a statement, or a quote—related to the lesson topic. This draws learners into the lesson even before the lesson begins. Learning should begin when a person enters the room. It can be called "covert" learning because it takes place even while people are greeting each other, getting their coffee, and talking about their week and other preliminary matters.
- Remove all old posters from previous lessons from the focal wall except the unit overview. Make sure that the focal wall is not too busy.
- You don't have to have walls to have Sunday School. All you need is the learners' attention. The goal is to create readiness to learn. While a wall can't do this, a visual and a well-prepared teacher can.
- Make sure whatever space you meet in is as clean as possible.

Chairs
- Provide enough chairs for class members plus any guests. Always have more chairs than participants. Practice the empty chair principle: place empty chairs in the room to represent the fact that the class needs to be reaching new people.
- Evaluate the best way to set up chairs. Chairs can create barriers or they can invite interaction. Regimented rows are probably the most difficult chair setup for interaction and relationship building. A semicircle is probably the most effective. If your room isn't large enough for one row in this design, consider multiple rows using this configuration.
- Consider changing the chair arrangement from time to time.

Tables
- Avoid using tables if they create a barrier between you and others. Tables can sometimes inhibit building relationships.
- Don't use tables if they keep you from adding people. People are more important than arrangements.
- If tables are used, there should be enough room for everyone. Excluding people from a table due to space creates a barrier to effective Bible study.
- Consider using tables if you have adults with physical disabilities.

Enjoy the Session
Create a warm, friendly environment
- Make sure everyone receives a warm welcome. Encourage fellowship by modeling it. Get someone to help you welcome people as they arrive.
- Encourage everyone to wear a name tag. Provide permanent name tags if possible. Select a location where people can get their nametags as they enter the room.

Welcome Guests
- Greet people at the door.
- Use name tags each week, not just at the beginning of the year.
- Enlist someone as a "designated plant" to greet people and to help guests feel comfortable during and after the session.
- Enlist someone to register guests so follow-up can take place.
- Welcome guests sometimes during the session, but take care not to embarrass them.

Present the Lesson
- At some point the session must transition from fellowship to the lesson. You can use the focal wall display to help with this transition. It may include a time when individuals share thoughts or experiences with each other. Life Connections provides "Ice Breakers" that help facilitate this.
- Use the outline you prepared to present the lesson. Teach confidently, knowing that you have done your best to prepare and that God will bless and use you. Be sensitive to God's leading as He works in the lives of learners.
- Recognize the difference between biblical discussions and God's moving in the lives of people. Be flexible as God leads during the session, but don't get sidetracked. Be so familiar with the plan and direction that you can adjust your plans to His at any moment.
- Note in the margin of your plan the approximate time you expect to make each transition. This will ensure that you have ample time to challenge class members to accountability before the session ends.

Take Prayer Requests
Prayer requests are vital but can dominate the Sunday School session. Continue to evaluate the effectiveness of the class prayer time. Make sure that prayer time doesn't focus only on physical aches and pains or become a gossip session.

Teach the group how to pray for the lost, members-in-service, the mission of the class, new class starts, the church, country, and other important matters.

Determine the best way to gather prayer requests. You might try one of these.
- Use a prayer sheet such as the one available on the *Essentials for Excellence: Connecting Sunday School to Life* CD-ROM.
- Write prayer requests in a notebook as learners enter.
- Write the requests on a board.

Then have one person read the entire list to the class.

Use the prayer time wisely so that there is adequate time for effective Bible study. Prayer requests can provide a good transition between the fellowship time and the lesson. Or they can be a good way to end the session.

Some classes provide a time for their Care Groups to meet at the end of the Sunday School session. Care Groups are smaller groups within one Sunday School class that enable a class to focus on the ministry needs of individuals. They could meet with their leader or facilitator and pray together for one another at the end of a session. Sometimes leaders "debrief" the lesson during Care Group time. The *Life Connections Leader Guide* includes a time entitled "Caring Time" that is designed to support this approach.

CHAPTER 6

WHAT HAPPENS AFTER THE SESSION?

If we think that the lesson is the only reason that we teach, then we have been deceived. Do you and I think that 52 hours per year (52 sessions) of lessons are going to make a difference unless there's a connection to our weekly activities? God has called us to see lives *trans*formed, not just *in*formed. So let's end where we began. Sunday School is about change—transformational change. We can't stop at the end of the session.

At the same time we begin getting ready for next week's lesson, we are encouraging learners to apply the Bible study to their daily lives and to involvement in ministry. What are some ways we can do that?

- *Learner Guides.* Help learners understand how to use the *Learner Guide* during the week. Send reminders about study in the *Learner Guide*. Give simple assignments from the *Learner Guide* during the week. Call for responses from the lesson that was to be studied in the *Learner Guide* during the week.
- *Devotional Guides.* Emphasize the use of *Open Windows*, *Stand Firm*, *Journey*, or devotions from *HomeLife*, *Christian Single Plus*, or *Mature Living* as an encouragement to learners to continue in God's Word during the week.
- *Ministry during the week.* Provide prayer updates during the week either by phone, through a prayer ministry coordinator, or through Care Groups, prayer chains, or e-mail. Determine ways to involve members in the mission and work of the class.

Make visits and contacts each week with prospects and members who have specific needs. Encourage members who are always faithful with personal notes and letters of encouragement.

How to Help Adults Understand the Mission of Sunday School

Part of our work as leaders is to help adults see that they are on mission through Sunday School. It is not a place just to "absorb" but to prepare for service. Help adult learners understand how Sunday School should function. Review the following list to determine whether your class is functioning in all of these areas. If it isn't, lead your class to discuss ways in which they can be more functional.

- *Foundational*—Sunday School involves adults in doing the work of the Great Commission. It is an entry point for unbelievers and new believers. And it is foundational in helping believers to mature as they study God's Word and learn to serve.
- *Ongoing*—Sunday School meets regularly for Bible study and builds ongoing relationships with class members and prospects. There is a plan for ongoing ministry, outreach, and fellowship.
- *Evangelistic*—Sunday School's primary objective is to win the lost. There is a climate that encourages believers to invite, engage, and share Christ with the lost in class and beyond.
- *Focuses on Bible Study*—This is accomplished through ongoing small-group study as well as personal Bible study with the purpose of guiding adults toward conversion, maturity, and ministry.
- *Multiplies*—Sunday School challenges class members to discover their places of service as class leaders. As members mature, they are encouraged to serve elsewhere as leaders of youth, children, preschoolers, or adults. The group should anticipate the day when they will be able to start a new class.
- *Intentional*—Intentional planning and evaluation ensures that the class functions properly. Without intentionality, nothing happens except a lesson from week to week.

Which of these functions do you spend the majority of your time on as the teacher? If you are like me, the majority of your time is spent preparing for Bible study. We know that as stewards of God's Word, we must do a good job.

But we can't ignore the rest. Consider all we are to teach. Invite your members to join with with you as you teach one another how to minister by functioning fully as a Sunday School class. You need the class's help. God does not intend for a teacher or director to do all the ministry. You have the privilege of teaching to minister.

What Kind of Help Should I Look For?

Organization is vital to leading Adult Sunday School classes to function properly. But remember, organize with purpose. Don't just fill a chart with names of leaders. Also, don't just enlist leaders to help the class function. Remember the purpose for the class and the class leaders. Begin with some core leaders.

- **All classes need at least three leaders.**
1. *Teacher*—leads the total ministry of a class, which includes a lot more than a single hour of Bible teaching per week. The teacher is also a spiritual mentor. Until the rest of the leadership team is enlisted and trained, the entire ministry of a class rests on the shoulders of the teacher.

    Teachers can't lead classes to function as open groups by themselves. They need at least two additional leaders.
2. *Ministry Coordinator*—organizes and leads the leadership team and members in visitation/evangelism and ministry. As a basic class leader, the ministry coordinator might also keep records and register guests. As a class and its ministry needs grow, the ministry coordinator enlists and trains additional leaders. This leader becomes the key partner in helping the teacher lead the class to function with purpose—as an open group.
3. *Apprentice*—partners with the teacher to help the class function as an open group. This is more than a partnership. It is also mentoring. Apprentices aren't substitutes, but learners. The teacher guides the apprentice to learn how to lead an effective Adult Sunday School ministry. Eventually, the apprentice is sent out to begin a new class.

- **As leaders are developed and the class grows, expand the leadership.** Consider the following leaders as you expand:
1. *Visitation/Evangelism Coordinator*—enlists members to discover, visit, contact, and develop relationships with prospects. This leader also trains class members to share their faith. If a church participates in the FAITH Sunday School Evangelism Strategy® then this person coordinates the work of the class FAITH Team(s).
2. *Care Group Leaders:* Each of these leaders minister to four to six members and members-in-service. Every member needs regular encouragement in good times and in times of crisis. These leaders provide the means for ongoing ministry to those who have moved out of the class and into service. Care group leaders multiply ministry far beyond what an individual leader could accomplish.

- **If a class has effectively developed leaders, consider enlisting additional leaders to help with the following ministry responsibilities.**
1. *Fellowship Coordinator*—enlists members to create and plan enjoyable activities and events that foster closer friendships within the class.
2. *Prayer Coordinator*—works with the teacher and apprentice to encourage personal and spiritual growth beyond the classroom. This growth includes prayer, devotional life, Family Bible Time, and involvement in discipleship courses.
3. *Missions Coordinator*—leads the class to participate in mission through involvement, prayer, and giving.

Find additional supporting resources that will help on the CD-ROM included in the book, *Essentials for Excellence: Connecting Sunday School to Life* by Louis Hanks and Alan Raughton.

Chapter 7

FOR ADULTS WITH SPECIAL NEEDS

Leaders who work in special-needs Sunday School face many challenges. Individual learning abilities vary greatly from member to member. Mobility issues—classroom location, room setup, and bathroom facilities—affect class member attendance in all activities. Consider transportation needs as well.

The *PREPARE, ENCOUNTER, AND CONTINUE* model is an effective ministry tool for reaching persons with disabilities for Christ.

PREPARE (Before the Session)
Study the lesson for personal growth using the Personal Bible Study section of the Leader Guide to enrich your walk with God. Use the *Access Leader Guide* with the anticipation that God has a message for you.

Identify the Biblical Truth to share with students. While creativity and variety help address individual learning styles, don't neglect the main biblical concept. Every lesson and activity should clearly present this message.

Gather resources which will create excitement for learning and help present the Biblical Truth in clear and understandable ways. Plan in advance for role play, object lessons, posters, games, and activities. For help, use the preparation checklist in the *Access Leader Guide*, plus the CD-ROM and material in the *Access Leader Pack*.

ENCOUNTER (During the Session)
Reinforce the biblical truth at each step of the teaching plan. Students may leave excited about what they did in class but not realize how each part fits together. They may miss the intended life change.

Lead the Bible study in creative ways. It is important to use learning activities that connect every student to the message of the Scriptures. All people, including those with special needs, have learning styles that influence how they learn. The teaching plan in the *ENCOUNTER* portion of the *Access Leader Guide* provides a variety of methods that you may use to meet the needs of your students:
• Relational—role play, dialogue, interview
• Musical—singing, tapes, musical presentations
• Logical—lecture, outline, written assignments
• Natural—outside walk, reflect upon creation
• Physical—games, art activities, sing with motions
• Visual—charts, posters, object lesson, drawings
• Verbal—storytelling, news story, testimonies
• Reflective—creative writing, journal, case study

Teach for transformation. Teachers in special needs classes must be willing to do just that—teach. Persons with disabilities can learn, hear the gospel, and grow in a relationship with Christ.

Teach with excitement. Let the transforming message of Christ's love manifest itself through your actions. Facial expressions, hand movements, and your tone of voice will guide some students to a better understanding of the lesson.

CONTINUE (After the Session)
Commitment to lead in a special-needs class requires one important component—relationship.

Send activity sheets home with class members to create an open avenue for students to live the lesson throughout the week. Parents or caregivers can help reinforce Sunday School lessons and Bible truths.

Stay in touch. Class members appreciate receiving mail or phone calls when they have been absent or when they celebrate a special event. Make personal visits to create relationships. Leaders who visit class members at home, at work, or at a special event, send the message loud and clear, "I care about you!" to members, their families, and caretakers.

Communicate regularly through weekly or monthly information in the church newsletters or bulletin. Provide information about activities for families and create awareness among the church body.

Teachers of special needs classes make the greatest difference when they *PREPARE, ENCOUNTER*, and *CONTINUE*.

By Marci Campbell, Special Education Specialist, LifeWay Christian Resources, Nashville, Tennessee, and Carlton McDaniel, Jr., a leader in the special education ministry of Highland Baptist Church, Raleigh, North Carolina.

Procedures

TEACHING PROCEDURES

Session Goal
This 2.5 hour plan is designed for use in a local church to help teachers prepare for the Sunday session using LifeWay Sunday School curriculum. You may adapt this plan for a shorter time frame if necessary. Additional helps and an expanded teaching plan for Association or State training is available at *www.lifeway.com/downloads*.

Preparation
Read the entire book before the session so you can become familiar with the content.
- Prepare the room by arranging chairs in a semicircle.
- Write the following quote on a poster or large marker board and display it on the focal wall: "Maximum learning is always the result of maximum student involvement, for we always learn by doing."—Howard Hendricks
- On the focal wall, prepare and display three posters with the following information:
  Poster #1:
  Title: Begin Sunday Afternoon or Monday.
  Outline: Evaluate; Set Weekly Goals; Overview Next Week's Lesson.
  Poster #2:
  Title: Study the Lesson.
  Outline: Daily Increments; Devotionally; Analytically; Commentary; Prayer, Additional Resources.
  Poster #3:
  Title: Crafting the Lesson.
  Outline: Key #1: Plan with the end in mind; Key #2: Customize!; Seven Steps to Customizing the Lesson; Develop an Outline.
- Although curriculum excerpts are provided, it is recommended that teachers bring or be given the LifeWay curriculum they use in Sunday School. Each will need the *Leader* and *Learner Guides* during the training session.
- If your church budget prohibits you from providing all the resources mentioned in the book, consider ordering a display of some of the resources and give leaders information on how they can order materials on their own if they so desire.
- The last chapter discusses Adult Sunday School leadership positions. If your church recommends different titles and/or roles for leaders in Adult Sunday School, customize the presentation of this content to meet the needs of your church.

Procedures
1. *Learning Debate.* Invite participants to read the quote by Howard Hendricks. Explain that they will debate either for or against the statement. Instruct those who disagree to stand on one side of the room. Invite those who totally agree with the statement to stand on the other side. Have fun with the debate.

   Some will try to relate this to learning styles, but it is really about the result of learning. Remain neutral as they debate. As they debate, ask questions such as: "Would you fly in a plane with someone who scored a perfect score on a written test about flying, but had never flown a plane?" or "Would you ride in a car with a 16-year-old who scored a perfect score on the written portion of a driver's education test but had never driven?" Explain that the goal of learning is change.

2. *Why Do You Teach?* Use the content from the introduction to challenge teachers to teach for change. Conclude by reading and explaining the process of change pictured in 2 Timothy 3:14-17. Explain that the goal of the session is to help teachers intentionally prepare for a Sunday session that leads adults to change.

3. *Begin Sunday afternoon or Monday.* Refer to Poster #1 and invite participants to turn to chapter 2 in their books as you overview the main points of the chapter. Use the poster outline to keep participants focused on the discussion. As you present the material in chapter 2, invite participants to stop and answer some of the questions. Provide time for discussion.

4. *Study the Lesson.* Refer to Poster #2 and chapter 3 and repeat the process you used in step 3.

5. *Crafting the Lesson.* Refer to Poster #3 and chapter 4 and repeat the process you used in step 3.

6. *Experiencing God During the Session.* Ask participants to read through chapter 5 on their own. Ask them to circle items that they need to incorporate into the Sunday Session. Provide a time to discuss your leaders' classroom needs.

This is a good stopping point if you are not teaching the entire 2.5 hour teaching plan. If you conclude at this point, go directly to Step 8 and close in prayer. Challenge leaders to go to their rooms and begin setting up their room based on what they discovered in this chapter.

7. *What Happens After the Session?* Invite participants to turn to chapter 6. Briefly emphasize the following points contained in chapter 6:
   - Learning doesn't end at the end of the session. How do we continue learning?
   - How do we help adults understand the mission of Sunday School?

Review the points related to "How to Help Adults Understand the Mission of Sunday School" and ask the group to circle the characteristic that reflects their class's greatest weakness and its greatest strength. Discuss their findings.

Then ask them to place an asterisk beside the item they spend the most time on each week—most likely this will be "Focuses on Bible Study." Emphasize the fact that we must be good stewards of the teaching of God's Word, so this is natural. But the other points must be a part of an effective Sunday School class as well. Explain that you can't do all of this on your own. You need help.
   - How do you get adults to help join you in the mission of Sunday School?

Provide an overview of the section, "What Kind Of Help Should I Look For?" If your church has a different list of adult class leaders or different titles, be sure to customize this overview to the specific needs of your church. Provide time for participants to determine the kinds of leaders they'll need to begin developing for their class to continue to function beyond the session.

8. *Conclusion.* Invite participants to turn to the "Doer of the Word—A Paraphrase of James 1:22-25" on this page. Read James 1:22-25 from the Bible and then invite someone to read the paraphrase. Close by challenging the group to go lead adults toward change that helps them become "doers" and not "hearers only."

Doer of the Word
A Paraphrase of James 1:22-25

Lead adults to be doers of the word and not hearers only.

Those who hear the word but don't become doers of the word think they have learned but have been deceived.

They think if they receive a good outline and experience a great presentation that they have learned.

They come and they study God's Word each week, but it makes no difference in how they live during the week. They forget what they study.

It is like looking in a mirror and then forgetting what you look like.

They come to Bible study, open the mirror of God's Word for one hour, and they see what manner of men they really are.

But when they leave, they don't continue to look in the mirror of God's Word during the week. They soon forget what they learned.

Those who look into the mirror of God's Word—through Bible study, prayer, and practice—are doers of the Word and will be blessed in all they do.

They will not quickly forget what God has said, but they will grow to become the people God intends for them to be.

Their continued look into the mirror of God's Word will change how they relate to others and will motivate them to seek out avenues of service.

--John McClendon

Permission is granted to reproduce for use in a local church.

CHRISTIAN GROWTH STUDY PLAN

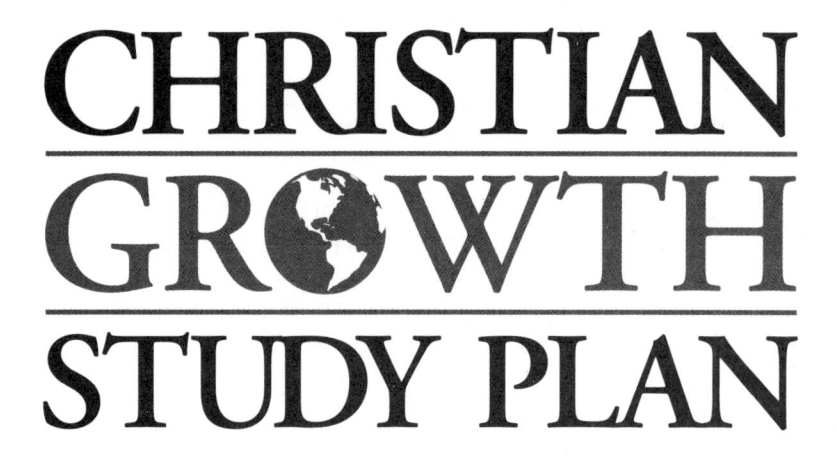

In the Christian Growth Study Plan (formerly Church Study Course), this book *HOW-TO SUNDAY SCHOOL GUIDE: CURRICULUM WORKSHOP FOR ADULT LEADERS* is a resource for course credit in the Leadership and Skill Development plans. To receive credit, read the book, complete the learning activities, show your work to your pastor, a staff member or church leader, then complete the following information. This page may be duplicated. Send the completed page to:

Christian Growth Study Plan
One LifeWay Plaza
Nashville, TN 37234-0117
FAX: (615)251-5067
Email: cgspnet@lifeway.com

For information about the Christian Growth Study Plan, refer to the Christian Growth Study Plan Catalog. It is located online at www.lifeway.com/cgsp. If you do not have access to the Internet, contact the Christian Growth Study Plan office (1.800.968.5519) for the specific plan you need for your ministry.

How-To Sunday School Guide: Curriculum Workshop for Adult Leaders
Course Number: LS-0036 Adult Sunday School Leadership

PARTICIPANT INFORMATION

Social Security Number (USA ONLY-optional) | Personal CGSP Number* | Date of Birth (MONTH, DAY, YEAR)

Name (First, Middle, Last) | Home Phone

Address (Street, Route, or P.O. Box) | City, State, or Province | Zip/Postal Code

Please check appropriate box: ❑ Resource purchased by self ❑ Resource purchased by church ❑ Other

CHURCH INFORMATION

Church Name

Address (Street, Route, or P.O. Box) | City, State, or Province | Zip/Postal Code

CHANGE REQUEST ONLY

❑ Former Name

❑ Former Address | City, State, or Province | Zip/Postal Code

❑ Former Church | City, State, or Province | Zip/Postal Code

Signature of Pastor, Conference Leader, or Other Church Leader | Date

*New participants are requested but not required to give SS# and date of birth. Existing participants, please give CGSP# when using SS# for the first time. Thereafter, only one ID# is required. **Mail to:** Christian Growth Study Plan, One LifeWay Plaza, Nashville, TN 37234-0117. Fax: (615)251-5067.

Rev. 3-03